The Wo

Beginners

Second Edition (Revised)

A Vermiculture Starter

Or

How to Be a Backyard Worm Farmer

And

Make The Best Natural Compost

Frank Randall

@BackyardFarmBks
facebook.com/BackyardFarmBooks
backyardfarmbooks.com

ISBN: 1482609207
ISBN-13: 978-1482609202

DEDICATION

To backyard owners everywhere -
whether a farmer in your heart or just your dreams.

CONTENTS

1

WORM BIOLOGY 101

Although some people may not be thrilled with the concept of raising worms, most good gardeners love the idea. That's because worms are like Mother Nature's recycling center. They feed on bacteria attached to the world's scraps and leftovers and the resulting worm manure (or castings) is rich in nutrients.

Worm composting, also called vermicomposting or vermiculture, is especially popular in areas where soil quality may not be the best. Keeping a worm box and making your own nutrient-rich soil can be the difference between having a few sickly plants in your yard or growing a beautiful garden full of vegetables and flowers.

Worm Anatomy

Worm anatomy is actually quite interesting. First of all, worms have segmented bodies, which enable them to move across the ground. Their movement is similar to a person climbing rocks; one segment will "grab" some soil using small hairs and the other segments will swing around and grab another clump of soil to move forward.

It's the ability of each segment to individually grip the soil that makes the worm appear to wiggle as they move. It also gives the worm complete flexibility and the ability to even bend backwards if needed, like a snake striking at prey.

The Head Segments

Each body segment of a worm has certain functions assigned to it. Segments one through five contain the mouth, brain, and pharynx. Worms have no eyes, but they can sense light and dark thanks to light sensitive tissue on their head. Since they prefer the dark, worm composters leave the lid of a worm box open, because the light causes the worms to burrow further down into the dirt pile, in turn making them more productive.

The Circulation Segments

There are three main vessels that supply the blood to a worm's organs: the aortic arches and the dorsal and ventral blood vessels. There are five pairs of aortic arches, which work like a heart, pumping blood into the dorsal and ventral blood vessels. The dorsal vessels carry blood to the front of the worm's body, and the ventral vessels carry blood to the back. The worm's aortic arches are located in segments 6 through 10.

Intestinal, Respiratory and Reproductive Segments

The digestive system is located in segments 11 through 20, and is comprised of a pharynx, esophagus, crop, intestine, and the gizzard. A worm's mouth has an attached appendage, or wedge, that pushes food into the mouth. Worms don't have teeth to chew so food is swallowed by the pharynx. It then passes through the esophagus and into the crop where it is stored. Eventually, the food will move into the gizzard, where small stones swallowed by the worm will grind the food, before sending it along to the intestines. Digestive fluids in the intestines break down the food even more so it can be absorbed by blood vessels in the intestinal walls.

Segments 11 through twenty 20 also control a worm's respiratory system. Instead of lungs, there is a layer of moist cells that diffuse oxygen and carbon dioxide.

Adult worms use part of their last segment areas for reproduction. Worms are hermaphrodites, meaning they can function as both male and female. However, contrary to popular belief, most worm species cannot reproduce on their own – this process is called parthenogenesis. The types of worms that you need for composting, require other worms to reproduce.

During the mating process, a ring called the clitellum forms around the worm, which will then back out of the ring, creating a fertilized cocoon. Each cocoon will incubate around two to three weeks. Then the egg capsules hatch, releasing new worms.

Each egg capsule can create anywhere from two to twenty new worms, so it can be difficult to accurately estimate how many worms you will have as time passes. However, studies suggest the average is four to five worms per egg.

Life Span and Population Growth

Worms can live up to 20 years. Since they multiply quickly you should expect considerable population growth. It is generally a good idea to start composting with only a small amount of worms, and then sit back and watch the population grow.

When to Feed the Worms

Worms can't survive on the same small box of soil forever, and will tell you when it's time to feed them some new soil. The worms will start at the bottom of the compost pile and work their way up, so simply change the soil when they get to the surface or just below it.

You may have decided to take up worm composting in order to help your garden grow, or to do your part to protect the planet. However, you can also get a great deal of enjoyment just watching the worms work, because the vermicomposting process is really quite remarkable to experience.

2

WHAT KIND OF WORMS SHOULD I USE AND HOW MANY WILL I NEED?

If you want to start composting with worms, you're going to need a composting box, bedding, food, and a few other minor things. The vital component in worm composting, of course, is the worms themselves.

Selecting Your Worms

Avoid getting regular night crawlers, which are the worms found in most gardens. They don't normally eat organic waste, and they don't do well in the warm temperatures that are usually present in a compost box.

One of the best and most popular composting worms available is *Eisenia fetida*, the red worm, also known as:

- ☐ Red wigglers
- ☐ Tiger worms
- ☐ Brandling worms
- ☐ Manure worms

Unlike an average night crawler, red worms can withstand a wide range of temperatures, from 32° to 95° F (0° – 35° C). It's best for the worm box to be at the warmer end of the temperature range, which encourages the worms to dig down deeper into the soil where they act as recycling centers, and turn the waste materials into compost.

Another option is the European night crawler, *Eisenia hortensis*. They are also referred to by other names, including:

- Euros
- Belgian night crawlers
- ENCs

As the name suggests, *Eisenia hortensis* is more popular in Europe, but it is gaining a following in North America as well. However, some studies suggest they aren't quite as efficient as red worms, and don't reproduce as quickly either. But there are plenty of people who compost with worms that don't report a noticeable difference between the two species, so it really is a personal choice.

Determining How Many Worms You Need to Start

How many worms you need and the number of composting bins you will need to start with, depends on your situation and requirements, including the amount of waste material you want to compost, and the timescale in which you want your compost produced.

Most experts suggest that the most efficient composting ratio is one to two pounds of worms for every pound of waste you want to process. (The efficiency of your worm composting will be affected by other factors such as climate and the exact materials your waste consists of). If you have multiple composting bins, you may need to adjust your ratios accordingly.

Reproduction and Survival

As covered in Chapter One, worms reproduce quite rapidly and a population can double in less than three months. The exact rate depends on the type of worm, the availability of food, space and the temperature in the compost bin. While you can't predict exactly how many new worms will appear or exactly when, it's a possibility that you may end up with more worms than you want or need at some point. Your options will be to start new composting bins, sell your excess worms, or give them away to friends and family who are also interested in worm bin composting. What you don't want to do is release the extra worms into your garden. Red and European composting worms are not like your average garden worms; they need soil rich in waste materials so they will probably not survive in your garden for very long.

The Adjustment Period

Even though worms can multiply quickly, you shouldn't expect them to reproduce to their maximum potential from the start, as it takes a while for worms to adjust to their new environment. So if you want immediate rapid results, you should acquire additional worms to give your composting a kick start, rather than waiting for them to reproduce naturally.

Starting Slowly

As you can see, vermiculture can be complicated because worms can be a bit unpredictable. So when you are first starting out you need to be careful and patient. It's best to begin with one small worm bin. Keep the bin warm, and replace the fresh castings (compost made by the worms) with new waste material on a regular basis, so they will always have plenty of food.

If you follow those simple steps, you'll soon see your worms adjust to the new bin, start to reproduce, and turn your waste into the perfect garden fertilizer. After that, there are no limits to how far you could take your vermiculture!

3

WHERE SHALL I PUT MY WORM BIN AND WHAT CONTAINER SHOULD I USE?

If you have now decided that you are ready to start your home worm composting bin, you need to know the right sort of container to choose, and just where to keep it.

Outdoor Insulation

Most people decide to keep their worm composting bins outside. There's nothing wrong with that, but there are several things to consider when you are positioning the bin. For example, red worms like temperatures that are at least above 40° F (5° C). Bins kept between 60° – 80° F (15° – 26° C) are usually the most efficient. If you live in a cold environment, you will need to insulate your worm bin by covering the lid and top layer of compost, with straw. You can also surround the bin with straw bales, for an extra coating of breathable, natural insulation.

Outdoor Weather and Moisture

Red worms like damp environments and breathe best in wet conditions. Imagine a sponge that has been wrung out; that's at least how wet your worm bin should be. However you need to be careful not to get the bin too wet; anything more than 75 percent moisture content can cause your composting bin to smell. If the climate in your area is fairly damp, you shouldn't have any problems, but if you live in a dry area, you will need to keep the worm bin suitably moist by simply adding a little water, as needed.

Outdoor Traffic

Another thing to consider is outdoor traffic. You need to care for your worms on a regular basis so you should keep the bin in an area that you or your family members walk by often. If the worms are right in front of you, it'll be easier remembering to feed and care for them.

Sheds and Outbuildings

You can also keep your worm bin in a shed or outbuilding to protect it from hot days and animal invaders. It can also offer you more control over your compost bin. However, the shed or outbuilding should not be too far away from the house, otherwise it can become easy to forget to check on your worms.

Indoor Considerations

There's absolutely nothing wrong with keeping your worm bin inside your home – but quite a few worm composters (or more often their partners!) are a little too squeamish. You could keep your bin under the sink, in the pantry, or anywhere else that is convenient, yet out of the way. The only reason that most people keep worm bins outside is that they are afraid of the worms getting loose in the house. However, that shouldn't happen if you have a bin with a secure lid. Whether you keep the worms inside or outside, you should keep a waste bucket in your kitchen for the whole family to put their food scraps in. Then, as the bucket fills, you can give it to the worms.

The Type of Bin

The worm bin itself should be made out of a secure material. Keep in mind that a sturdy bin isn't automatically a good bin for vermiculture. Metal bins are sturdy, but should be avoided due to potential harmful chemical reactions between the waste products or soil and the metal itself. So should any bins made from any sort of treated lumber or woods that are toxic to the worms, such as black walnut and cedar. Equally you should avoid using a cardboard box as the moisture from the soil can break down the box and the worms can work their way right through it.

The best type of bin is a sturdy plastic container, which you can buy in most hardware or department stores. Just make sure that it has a tight-fitting lid and is at least twelve inches wide and eight inches deep.

Pay Attention to Surface Area

The surface area within your worm bin is another important factor. A greater surface area allows for better oxygen flow, which will help your worms to stay active and process waste more efficiently. This is why you should never use a small bucket as a permanent worm bin, although it will work on a very temporary basis.

Adapting Your Bin

Once you have found your bin, you will need to adapt it for it's new inhabitants. You should drill several 1/8" to 1/2" in the bottom of the bin and the lower portions of the bin's sides for airflow. As well as letting air in and out, these holes mean that your worms could potentially escape! You will need to cover them with some fine mesh screen, affixed with non-toxic glue, to keep your worms safe and secure.

Prepare For Drainage

These holes in the worm bin don't just allow for airflow, they also allow excess moisture to escape. The best way to prepare for that is to place a tray of slightly larger dimensions than the bin underneath, to catch the runoff. Then, when required, simply empty the liquid from tray onto your flowerbed or plants – don't what ever you do just throw it down the sink! This is valuable and nutrient and microbe packed liquid fertilizer, referred to as 'tea'.

You may even find it beneficial to get two identical trays per bin so you can immediately swap a fresh tray for the full one to avoid any possibility of leakage. Check on your drainage tray every time you check on your worms, and you should have no problems.

Buying a Dedicated Worm Compost Bin

If you have slightly bigger budget, you can spend a few dollars more and purchase a dedicated worm composting bin system. That way you'll have optimized airflow and will avoid any leaks. Head over to **backyardfarmbooks.com/bins** for a list of tried and tested solutions.

The Right Bin

The right bin can go a long way towards ensuring that your worms are happy, healthy, and useful to you. As long as you remember that your worms are not entirely self-sufficient creatures — they are going to need your help in order to survive. Check on them frequently and give them what they need, and in return they'll reward you with excellent organic compost.

4

HOW DO I SETUP AND MAINTAIN MY WORM BIN?

The proper setup and maintenance of the bin will ensure that your worms are happy, healthy, and composting efficiently.

Bedding

Your worms are going to need some sort of bedding that is also safe for them to eat, since they will probably consume quite a large amount of it. There are many options, including leaf mold, peat moss or corrugated cardboard, but one of the most ecological, available and suitable choices is newspaper – as long as you follow these steps:

- ☐ Only use the black and white sections, never the colored pages
- ☐ Thoroughly shred the paper
- ☐ Soak it well and then squeeze out as much of the moisture as you can before adding it your bin

The important things to remember are that the bedding should be shredded, damp, fluffy (to allow for air flow) and, most importantly, not toxic to the worms. The bedding should fill about 2/3 of the worm bin. You should then add some fine dirt, soil, sand or finely crushed eggshells to the bedding, for the worms to consume as an aid to their digestion.

The Worms

Once the bedding is in place, it's time to add the worms. However many you add, be sure to give them enough space, as every pound of worms takes up about two cubic feet in a bin.

Be very careful when adding the worms, as they won't survive long when they are on the surface of the bedding. Hollow out an area about halfway down in the wet bedding, add the worms, and then replace the rest of the bedding on top and cover them up well. The other option that some people do is to place your worms on the top of the bedding and allow their own natural tendencies to take over. Shine a direct light source on them, so they burrow down into the bedding to escape. Just be sure that they do so relatively quickly - if not, you might have to give them a helping hand.

To be honest I find it just as easy, and kinder on the worms to use first method, but I am not at all squeamish about handling any insects, invertebrates or any other critters.

Adding Food to the Bin

Give your worms a day to adjust to their new surroundings before adding any food to the bin. After that only add food once or twice per week; worms don't like to be constantly disturbed.

Their food should consist mainly of fruit and vegetable rinds and peelings. You can also add crushed eggshells, plant clippings, coffee grounds and filters, used tea and tea bags and similar items. However, you must not add any meat, fish, oils, or dairy products, as these will soon attract rats, mice, raccoons and even bears and wolves — depending on where you live!

A pound of red worms can usually consume about five pounds of food scraps per week, but do be careful not to over feed your worms. If they are getting overwhelmed, hold off on adding new food until the previous batch has been thoroughly consumed.

It is imperative that when you add food to the bin, you are sure to place it beneath the surface of the bedding. Doing so should help to prevent fruit flies from invading your bin, and will also help to keep the odors under control.

Maintaining the Bin

Maintaining the bin is relatively easy. Periodically check the bedding in the bin - if too much of it is consumed, add a bit more. If the bedding seems too soggy, add a bit of dry bedding to the mix, and this will keep your worms happy.

You will also need to harvest both your tea, (the liquid that drips into the tray), and the castings (compost) in the bin. Do so as necessary, and be sure to replace any bedding that is lost in the process. As with the teas, the castings are nutrient packed wonderful natural fertilizer for your garden.

The most important thing to learn about worm bin maintenance is that you need to get to know your worms and their needs. Look out for problems in the bin and, if you find any, correct them quickly. That way, your worms will always produce great compost for you.

Frank Randall

5

WHAT DO I FEED MY WORMS?

One of the biggest challenges of composting with worms is that you need to know exactly what and how much the worms should be eating. Mixing in foods that are toxic to the worms, or that the worms simply don't like, will definitely prevent your compost bin from working efficiently.

Bedding as Food

Watch how much bedding is in the bin - if the worms are eating a lot of their bedding, you may not be adding enough kitchen scraps to keep them happy. If that's the case, try adding a few more scraps per week to the bin.

Good Scraps to Add

Worms love all kinds of vegetable, and grains like rice, pasta, oatmeal and healthy breakfast cereal make excellent compost scraps too. (Be sure that you don't include breakfast cereals that are high in sugar).

Here are some tips to remember:

Coffee and coffee grounds: An excess of these can make the bin too acidic for the worms; so don't add too much at any given time.

Bread: red mite can be attracted to surplus bread that has been left by the worms, so again add it in small quantities.

Onion, garlic, ginger, and potato skins: The worms will consume these foods very slowly, which can make your bin start to smell bad. Be sure to add these all I small amounts, and ensure they are buried below the surface of the bedding.

Scraps to Avoid Adding

There are some foods that should never be added to a vermicompost bin, such as oils, sugary snacks, potato chips, and candy. Some junk food can hurt or even kill the worms. Other junk food won't hurt the worms, but they just won't eat it, so it does no good in your composting bin.

A Note about Fruit

Avoid adding any food to the bin that contains a chemical called limonene, which is toxic to the worms. This is found in high concentrations in citrus fruits so avoid adding lemons, limes, grapefruit, oranges or similar fruits to your composting bin.

Nevertheless, worms do love a lot of fruits. Here are some options that are safe for them to eat:

- ☐ Apples
- ☐ Pears
- ☐ Peaches
- ☐ Melons
- ☐ Banana peel
- ☐ Strawberries and many other types of berries

Other Food Considerations

The worms also don't necessarily have to eat only kitchen scraps. For example, you might consider adding brown leaves, dead flowers, peat moss or plant clippings to your compost bin - all of those things are safe for the worms to eat.

On the other hand, do not add things like plastic, glass, or aluminum foil to a vermicomposting bin, along with other foreign objects, such as rubber bands, fruit bags or other non-biodegradable packaging.

A Note about Animal Feces

Animal feces, particularly dog and cat feces, should never be used as a fertilizer in a vegetable garden. So, you shouldn't put animal feces in your worm bin if you plan to use the castings to fertilize things that you may later eat. The worms will consume it; it's not harmful to them and can be used as fertilizer for plants that you are not going to eat. Some vermicomposters will have two separate worm bins – one for consuming scraps and producing fertilizer for their fruit and vegetables, and the other for consuming animal feces and scraps that will in turn produce fertilizer for their flower beds and non-fruit trees.

Make the Eating Process Easy

When you feed your worms, you should make the eating process easy for them. For instance, imagine if you were the size of a worm and someone dropped a whole apple into your home. Aside from potentially scaring you, you would probably be overwhelmed figuring out how to eat it! In other words, small worms require small food. So, the smaller you can shred, mash, or slice your waste materials, the better off the worms will be. Larger items will be consumed eventually, but they'll keep your composting bin from being as efficient as it could be.

Create a Feeding Schedule

Finally, it's important to create a feeding schedule for your worms. The exact schedule will depend on how many worms or worm bins you have. For one bin with one to two pounds of red worms, you will probably need to feed them once or twice a week. However, you should adjust the schedule, if you notice that the bin has too many food scraps or not enough. After a few weeks you will get to know your worms, and be better able to schedule feeding times and quantities.

6

HOW DO I TAKE CARE OF MY WORMS?

Worm composting can be a lot of fun, is great for the environment, and will also provide you with some wonderful organic fertilizer for your garden. However, you won't get very far unless you learn how to take care of your worms and keep them happy and productive.

Create a Secure Worm Bin

The first thing you can do for your worms is to create a secure worm bin. The bin should have a lid and be protected from predators, cold temperatures, direct sunlight and severe weather conditions.

Keep Air Flowing Through the Bin

As I mentioned before, your worm bin needs to have excellent airflow. As well as having ventilation holes in the bin itself, you need to ensure that the bedding and the scrap food in the bin is spread out and fluffy, rather than hard and compact.

Control Moisture

One of the most important aspects of taking care of your worms is that you absolutely have to control moisture in the worm bin. In some ways worms are like human beings. They have to stay hydrated because their bodies are largely composed of water. If the bin is too dry, your worms will die. However, there is a delicate balance that you need to maintain. If the bin becomes clogged and waterlogged, the worms will suffocate, and the food scraps will begin to rot and stink. Therefore, it's your job to make sure that the bedding material stays wet enough, but not too wet.

It's a good idea to check the top, middle and bottom layers of your worm bin frequently. If you notice too much moisture during your check, add some dry bedding to the mix. If, on the other hand, the bin is far too dry, add some wet bedding or wet food scraps to the bin. Most vermiculture enthusiasts recommend that you don't just pour water into your worm bin. It's not good for your worms or for the composting process, in general.

Proper Feeding

As well as sticking to the diet tips I discussed earlier, your worms need to be fed in specific ways. They can process food scraps quicker and more effectively if those scraps are small, so if in doubt, grind, shred, mash or blend the food.

Caring for the Worms at Different Times of Year

In the summer you should try to keep the worm bin in the shade, and give it a little extra damp bedding, as needed. In the winter, however, you should consider keeping the bin in the house or garage where it will be protected from the elements. You can also help it to stay healthy and active in the winter by taking some other steps. For example, if the bin is outside, you can insulate it further by adding dry bedding on top or surrounding it with straw bales. You can also blend all of the food for the worms in the winter, rather than leaving large items, such as banana peel, in the bin. That's because the microbial breakdown of the food will slow down in the winter, making it more difficult for the worms to process larger food items.

In the cold months, you may also want to consider keeping an external heat source near the worm bin. However, be sure to monitor the temperature of the bin closely. Baking your worms is not any better than freezing them!

For the most part, a worm bin takes care of itself, as long as you feed the worms properly, harvest the compost when it's appropriate, and keep the bin warm, moist and comfortable.

Worms are fairly resilient little creatures, so, you don't have to worry too much about keeping them alive in the winter. Instead, the focus should be on how to make them productive in the cold months as well as in the warm ones. If you follow the steps above, you should have no problem accomplishing that goal.

Frank Randall

7

COMMON PROBLEMS YOU MIGHT HAVE IN YOUR WORM BIN

This is without a doubt an enjoyable and useful hobby, but it's not always easy. Here are some potential problems you might encounter and ways to either or fix them quickly.

Temperature and Level of Moisture

As previously stated, the temperature of your worm bin is important. Your worms will do their best work at temperatures that are warm and comfortable, generally between 55 and 75 degrees Fahrenheit. If the bin is colder than that, the worms won't work efficiently. In addition to relocating or insulting with straw bales, you can use blanket, lamps and even heating pads.

However your worm bin is equally at risk if the temperature is too high. If this happens, the waste materials that you are trying to compost could rot or dehydrate, causing the bin to become useless, your worms could escape in their efforts to get away from the extreme heat (if your bin isn't properly constructed) and of course your worms could die.

If you need to cool down a bin you can move it to a shady or climate-controlled area. You can also make sure that the bin is properly ventilated to allow for ventilation. Lastly, you can place a tray of ice cubes inside the bin or use fans to help cool the bin off.

As discussed earlier, the level of wetness is another thing that can cause problems in a worm bin. Too much water can cause major problems for the worms and for your composting plans too. If your bin does seem to be getting too wet, you can fix that in a couple of easy ways.

Method one is to adjust the kinds of waste that you are putting into the bin. Try not to add food scraps that are too moist for a week or so. Some of the scraps to temporarily avoid are cucumber, melons, berries and tomatoes.

Method two is to decrease the dampness in the worm bedding itself. You can do that by adding in some dry bedding, such as shredded dry newspaper. Make sure to add some of this to the bottom of the bin, as liquid drains down and out in that direction. The new dry bedding will absorb some of the surrounding moisture and reduce the overall sogginess in the bin.

If your worm bin is actually too dry, simply do the opposite. So, try adding a few more wet foods and try adding some wet bedding to the bin. You can also take a spray bottle and lightly spray the top of the bin, but you shouldn't just dump water into the worm bin.

Another thing to remember is that dryness can indicate that your bin is too hot. So, you may want to check the temperature. Based on your findings, you can try to adjust the temperature of the bin to reduce the possibility of the bin becoming dry again.

Compost thermometers vary in cost from around $10 all the way up to $150, but are a vital tool to happy worms and efficient composting – plenty of info here **backyardfarmbooks.com/CP**

Bad Smells

Another common but easy to rectify problem in your worm bin is bad smells. An efficient worm bin should not ordinarily have a strong unpleasant aroma. If it does, it is probably due to one of the following reasons:

- ☐ The bin is too wet
- ☐ The food is rotting
- ☐ The food isn't buried beneath the surface
- ☐ You haven't given your worms the right food

If the problem is related to the food, you may need to make some changes to how you are feeding the worms. First of all, make sure that any scraps you add to the bin are buried just below the surface. Exposed waste materials will only attract pests and cause smells, and make sure the food is of the right type and the right size.

Escaping Worms

Worms aren't really known for being explorers. They don't like light sources and they generally like to stick to one place and one routine. So, if your worms are trying to escape, there's a problem in the bin such as it has become too wet, too acidic, or infested with some sort of pest.

To adjust for acidity, change what you are feeding the worms. Don't give them too many foods with high acid content. Your bin needs to have a pH in the 6.4 to 6.9 range, and this is easy to check with a simple tester – you can get one of these for just a few dollars. There is more info at **backyardfarmbooks.com/pH**

Most worm bin pests can be avoided if you keep your bin secure and the area around it clean, you bury the scraps below the surface and keep the temperature controlled. However, sometimes you can do all that and pests might still show up. If so, you can temporarily transfer your worms into a box, clean the bin well, and then start over with new bedding. That should take care of the pest problem.

As you can see, there are a lot of problems that can occur. However, as long as you take care of your worms properly, you shouldn't encounter most of them. Even if you do have problems, most of the solutions are simple. So, you can relax and enjoy vermicomposting!

8

WHAT ARE THESE OTHER CREATURES IN MY WORM BIN?

There are several other creatures that could "worm their way" into your bin. Most pose no threat to your worms, but that doesn't automatically make them good creatures to have in there!

Fruit Flies

Fruit flies and similar flying pests are usually attracted by exposed foods. Therefore, any foods added to your composting bin should be buried below the surface and covered up properly. You can also prevent flying invasions by keeping your worm bin lid closed and the area around your composting bin properly cleaned.

Fruit flies, as the name suggests, are often attracted to fruit. So, reducing the fruit you add to the bin can get rid of some of them. If that doesn't work, you can try hanging flypaper around the composting bin.

 A strong vacuum cleaner can also be used to suck up a lot of the flies in the air. You won't get rid of all of them, but you can keep their numbers under control and, hopefully, worry a bit less about being swarmed by fruit flies each time you check your worm composting bin. Just don't forget to empty the vacuum cleaner immediately afterwards! On the one occasion I forgot, vacuuming the house a couple of days subsequently was not a pleasant experience…

Red Mites and Friends

Another type of pest that you might see in the worm bin is a mite. They come in many varieties, but red mites are the most common. They are attracted to wet conditions and foods that contain a lot of water, such as melons and cucumbers.

On one hand, red mites won't hurt your worms. On the other hand, they can cause your worms to burrow down deeper in their bedding. That means that the worms won't be able to process the waste materials near the top of the bin.

White mites are also known to invade worm bins, but usually only when worms or other creatures are dying. They scavenge and eat dead creatures. So if you see white mites in your bin you may need to extract the worms and start a new, clean worm bin.

Another type of mite-like insect is the springtail, a jumping insect that reproduces at a very fast rate. Like red mites, they can force your worms into hiding at the bottom of the bin.

The best way to get rid of springtails and most types of mites in the bin is to try adding dry bedding and reducing the amount of wet foods added to the bin. As conditions dry out, the pests should give up and leave.

If that doesn't work, you can try attracting the pests to the top of the bin by wetting it. Then you can use a cigarette lighter or even carefully use a blowtorch to burn the pests away. Alternatively, you can use a vacuum cleaner to suck them up. However, you shouldn't use your household vacuum cleaner, for the very reason I mentioned earlier. Instead, get a vacuum that is meant for industrial purposes or you will be very unpopular (as I was with my wife).

Ants

Ants can eat all of the food and destroy your composting bin in no time at all. To avoid an ant infestation you have the following options

- ☐ Always keep the area around the bin clean
- ☐ Put your bin on legs and put each leg in a dish of water. Ants don't like large amounts of water and will be unable to climb up and into the worm's home
- ☐ Place ant traps around the bin

If ants do get into your bin you can usually scare them off by adding some soggy bedding to the area where you see them, as the water should force them to leave. Once they are gone, add dry bedding to get your moisture level back to normal. If that doesn't work, you may be able to scoop out the section of bedding where the ants are and replace it with new bedding.

Remember that it is the food scraps in the bin that are attracting the ants in the first place, so keep the worm food from becoming ant meals by ensuring that it is covered with bedding.

Rodents

Rodents can also be attracted to a worm bin, but they are usually attracted to the smell of rotting meat or dairy products. So, if you don't put any dairy products or meat in your bin, you probably won't see any rodents around it – simple!

If you're still concerned about rodents, put your bin on legs to make it harder to access. Also, make sure that it is well sealed, except for the small ventilation holes. If necessary, you can place rodent traps around the composting bin as well.

If you take the proper steps to keep your bin and the area around it clean and cared for, pests shouldn't be a problem. However, you should definitely watch for invasions and catch them early, if they do occur. A small problem with pests is usually easy to treat, but a major invasion may require you to start a brand new vermicomposting bin; not the end of the world, but something to avoid if possible.

9

WHEN AND HOW DO I HARVEST FROM MY WORM BIN?

Worm composting is a fun hobby, but there's a good chance that you are not doing it just for the fun and enjoyment. You probably started composting with worms to create some great fertilizer for your garden, so you have to know how and when to harvest the worm castings.

The Time Is Right

It's important to harvest the fertilizer when the time is right. Unfortunately, no two bins are alike! The readiness of the castings depends on a number of things, including bin size, the number of worms, the amount, type and size of food and the weather conditions.

The readiness of the castings also depends on how you plan to use them. For example, you don't have to be all that picky if you are just using the castings in your own home garden. You may have some larger bits of food in your compost, but you can use a bucket and a screen to sift those out. Therefore, you don't have to wait as long for good fertilizer.

On the other hand, you may be planning to sell or give away some of the compost that you make. If so, you should try to be a bit more patient. Don't harvest the castings from the worm bin until they have an even, rich, soil-like look.

The End Is Based on the Start

When it comes to vermicomposting, the end is based on the start. For example, if you use peat moss for bedding in the beginning, the finished castings will be dark and fluffy. Whereas castings from worms that had newspaper for bedding will be considerably less fluffy and much lighter in color.

Get to Know Your Bin

It can take anywhere from a few weeks to a few months for a bin to be ready for harvesting. So, it's very important for you to get to know your bin, do some research and learn to recognize the signs that the compost is ready.

Harvesting Tips and Tools

Knowing when to harvest your worm castings is only half of the issue; the other half is learning how to do so. To start, you will potentially be working with mold, bacteria, fungal spores, and other microorganisms, so if you are prone to allergies you should definitely wear gloves and a mask. You may also want to ask your doctor for other safety tips.

Next, you'll need the following tools:

- ☐ Large plastic bags
- ☐ A large plastic tray or other flat work surface
- ☐ One or more large buckets
- ☐ A scoop or spatula
- ☐ A garden fork
- ☐ Screens (if you plan to sift the compost)

Harvesting Method One: Dumping

There are two main ways to harvest your worm compost. The first is a simple matter of removing the top layer of unfinished food and bedding from the bin and then dumping the compost, worms and all, onto a large sorting tray under direct light.

Work the contents from the bin into large mounds of dirt on your tray. The worms, wanting to avoid the light source, will burrow deep into the mounds of dirt. Every few minutes you can scoop the top layer of castings off into a bucket. It should be worm-free, since all of the worms will be moving towards the bottom.

Once you only have worms left, weigh them so that you know how many there are. Then, put them back into the composting bin with fresh bedding. Remember that 1,000 worms weigh about a pound. That will help you to determine whether you should split some of the worms into a new bin.

Harvesting Method Two: Dividing

An alternative to dumping is dividing. You can control the worms' movements in the bin by where you feed the worms. So, you can place fresh bedding and food on one side and get the worms to go to that side. That will allow you to harvest the compost on the other side of the bin. However, do keep in mind that it may take the worms several weeks to migrate from one side of the bin to the other.

Saving the Cocoons

Worm cocoons are usually confined to the top six inches or so of a vermicomposting bin. If you want to save them, simply use a scoop to get them out. Pour each scoop over a fine mesh screen into a bucket. The cocoons should stay on the surface of the mesh screen and then you can move them into a new bin.

Harvesting the Tea

Finally, most worm bins have trays under them to catch the compost tea, which can be just as good a garden fertilizer as the worm castings. Although, contrary to what the name suggests, it does not make a good tea so you should never drink it! Harvesting compost tea is simple. Just take the tray out from under your vermicompost bin and pour the liquid in your garden. If you want, you can pour the compost tea directly into your castings after harvesting is complete. Then you can just sprinkle the castings in the garden. Either way, you should see some great results in your garden.

10

WHAT CAN I DO WITH THE CASTINGS AND VERMICOMPOST IN MY GARDEN?

Why is it that so many people are vermicomposting? Well, it all comes down to one thing: the compost is incredibly useful in the garden. Let's look at some of the things that vermicompost can do for your soil and plant growth.

Add Nutrients

While most gardeners are aware of the fact that plants need phosphorus, potassium and nitrogen, many overlook other nutrients. Although the plants may only need small amounts they are still important. Some of them include copper, iron, iodine, zinc, manganese, boron and cobalt.

Vermicompost contains all of those nutrients and more, which it releases to the plants on an as needed basis. When the plants are blooming and need more nutrients, they get them. During less active months, they get less of them. Your worm castings and the nutrients within work as a natural remedy because they can kill off harmful toxins in the soil, allowing your plants to grow up to be healthy and strong.

Improve Soil Structure

Another big benefit of worm compost is that it can create improved soil structure. For example, soil that is too sandy and compact doesn't allow for air or water flow and tends to be too dry and easily blown away by wind or washed away by rain. Vermicompost can hold water equal to double the dry weight of the compost. That means that the soil will be moist enough for the plants and a little clumpier, allowing it to withstand wind and rain. Soil like that can also help your plants to survive through droughts.

Balance the Acidity of the Soil

You can monitor the pH levels of your soil and add the right type of vermicompost to change those levels. Remember, the types of foods you use in your composting bin will have a direct impact on the pH levels of the finished compost. So, in a sense, worm composting can allow you to be a chemist or soil doctor.

Bring in New Life

Microorganisms, such as earthworms and insects, can feed on the nutrient-rich mixture in the castings, which can bring balance to the ecosystem in your garden. All the microorganisms attracted by the vermicompost can help your garden in many ways. They can dig holes, which promotes water drainage and air flow. Some of them feed on other unwanted garden pests. The existence of microorganisms in your garden is likely to attract other life, such as flying insects. Many of them, especially bees, can help with pollination. So, starting out with a small thing like the right organic compost can help your garden in immeasurable ways.

Simple Ways to Use Your Compost

There are a lot of ways to use your compost in the garden. One easy way is to simply use it as mulch for all of your vegetable and flowerbeds by sprinkling a layer of it evenly across the surface of your garden. The earthworms and other insects that live in the garden will then help the compost to be incorporated into the rest of the soil.

If you prefer to make sure that the compost gets all the way into the ground, you can do that, too. Simply take a small garden spade or shovel and hollow out a section of earth around your plants. Fill it with vermicompost and pat it into place with your hands or your spade, then, place the regular soil over the top of it.

More Specific Uses

There are also some more specific uses for vermicompost. For example, you can use it when you are planting new seeds by sprinkling the compost in the seed holes. That will give your seeds an excellent foundation for growth.

The same process can be done when you are transplanting seedlings to a new area: dig an appropriately sized hole and put the seedling in. Then, pack the excess space around the seedling with vermicompost. It's an easy way to give your seedlings the nutrients that they desperately need.

Another specific use for vermicompost is to create your own potting mix. You'll also need to incorporate water, regular soil, and some other elements. A potting soil based on organic compost is great for houseplants as well as potted seedlings that you plan to put into the garden at a later time.

Place and Time Don't Matter

The great thing about adding vermicompost to a garden is that place and time don't matter. You could add it to the soil in spring, summer, autumn, or even winter if you live in an area with little or no snow.

As long as you have been careful with the scraps you have fed your worms, you don't need to worry about using it on plants that will later be consumed by people because it is organic and healthy. A lot of chemical-based fertilizers can burn plants or pollute the surrounding area. They can also be quite hazardous to wildlife and pets so they should never be used in populated areas or near water sources. In fact, they should really never be used at all.

Luckily, you can do your part to protect the environment by using vermicompost in the garden. Not only that, but your vegetables are likely to grow bigger and taste better. Your flowers will be bigger and more beautiful. Considering all of those clear advantages, there's really no reason at all not to try vermicomposting.

CONCLUSION

I hope this book has given you an insight into worm composting, and helped you make up your mind as to if it is for you.

As I have done my best to summarize in this small book, vermiculture is fairly simple but still very rewarding and can be a unique part of your life, provide wonderful organic fertilizer for your garden and be a beneficial influence to the environment.

Best wishes,

Frank Randall
Ohio
September 2012

ABOUT THE AUTHOR

Frank was born and bred in Bradford, West Yorkshire, England, in 1945. Born into a family of mill workers, he spent much of his free time on the Yorkshire Moors feeding his fascination with wildlife and nature. He later went on to lecture at the BICC. In 1995 he immigrated to the USA and now lives in peace on the shores of Lake Erie, Ohio, with his wife, two dogs, a colony of honeybees, and a menagerie of other critters.

He's the author of Amazon's #1 Best Selling Backyard Farm Books, which include *The Bee Book for Beginners, The Worm Book for Beginners,* and *The Mushroom Book for Beginners* and *The Sustainable Living Book for Beginners.*

@BackyardFarmBks
facebook.com/BackyardFarmBooks
backyardfarmbooks.com

Frank Randall

YOUR FREE GIFT

To get your FREE copy of '**Butterfly Gardening**' just visit…

www.backyardfarmbooks.com/GoWB

…and sign up for my free newsletter.

If you have a minute to leave a review of '**The Worm Book for Beginners**' at Amazon that would be fantastic!

This URL will take you straight to the review page:

www.backyardfarmbooks.com/wrev

Many thanks.

ALSO FROM THIS AUTHOR

ALSO FROM THIS AUTHOR

Frank Randall

ALSO FROM THIS AUTHOR

Made in the USA
Monee, IL
07 February 2021

59875614R00033